My COUNTING BOOK

Text: Keith Faulkner   Illustration: Paul Johnson

WORLD INTERNATIONAL PUBLISHING LIMITED
MANCHESTER

This is Tilly Turtle.

She lives in the ocean and lays her eggs on the beach.

I wonder how many babies Tilly Turtle has?

Turn the wheel and count Tilly Turtle's babies.
Lift the flap and see if you are right.

This is Tammy Tiger.

She lives in the jungle and has a beautiful stripy coat.

I wonder how many babies Tammy Tiger has?

This is Penny Panda.

She lives in the forest and eats juicy bamboo shoots.

I wonder how many babies Penny Panda has?

This is Polly Parrot.

She flies above the jungle and makes her nest in a tree.

I wonder how many babies Polly Parrot has?

Turn the wheel and count Tammy Tiger's babies.
Lift the flap and see if you are right.

Turn the wheel and count Penny Panda's babies.
Lift the flap and see if you are right.

Turn the wheel and count Polly Parrot's babies.
Lift the flap and see if you right.

Now count all the babies from 1 to 10.

1 one

2 two

3 three

4 four

5 five